P9-DFU-525

FEB 2019

WOMEN
LEADING
THE WAY

Sonia Sotomayor

Supreme Court Justice

by Paige V. Polinsky

BLASTOFF!
2
READERS

BELLWETHER MEDIA • MINNEAPOLIS, MN

Note to Librarians, Teachers, and Parents:

Blastoff! Readers are carefully developed by literacy experts and combine standards-based content with developmentally appropriate text.

Level 1 provides the most support through repetition of high-frequency words, light text, predictable sentence patterns, and strong visual support.

Level 2 offers early readers a bit more challenge through varied simple sentences, increased text load, and less repetition of high-frequency words.

Level 3 advances early-fluent readers toward fluency through increased text and concept load, less reliance on visuals, longer sentences, and more literary language.

Level 4 builds reading stamina by providing more text per page, increased use of punctuation, greater variation in sentence patterns, and increasingly challenging vocabulary.

Level 5 encourages children to move from "learning to read" to "reading to learn" by providing even more text, varied writing styles, and less familiar topics.

Whichever book is right for your reader, Blastoff! Readers are the perfect books to build confidence and encourage a love of reading that will last a lifetime!

This edition first published in 2019 by Bellwether Media, Inc.

No part of this publication may be reproduced in whole or in part without written permission of the publisher. For information regarding permission, write to Bellwether Media, Inc., Attention: Permissions Department, 6012 Blue Circle Drive, Minnetonka, MN 55343.

Library of Congress Cataloging-in-Publication Data

Names: Polinsky, Paige V., author.
Title: Sonia Sotomayor : Supreme Court Justice / by Paige V. Polinsky.
Description: Minneapolis, MN : Bellwether Media, Inc., [2019] | Series: Blastoff! Readers: Women Leading the Way | Includes bibliographical references and index.
Identifiers: LCCN 2018033443 (print) | LCCN 2018033548 (ebook) | ISBN 9781681036694 (ebook) | ISBN 9781626179455 (hardcover : alk. paper) | ISBN 9781618915061 (pbk. : alk. paper)
Subjects: LCSH: Sotomayor, Sonia, 1954–Juvenile literature. | Hispanic American judges–Biography–Juvenile literature. | Judges–United States–Biography–Juvenile literature. | United States. Supreme Court–Officials and employees–Biography–Juvenile literature.
Classification: LCC KF8745.S67 (ebook) | LCC KF8745.S67 P65 2019 (print) | DDC 347.73/2634 [B] –dc23

LC record available at https://lccn.loc.gov/2018033443

Text copyright © 2019 by Bellwether Media, Inc. BLASTOFF! READERS and associated logos are trademarks and/or registered trademarks of Bellwether Media, Inc. SCHOLASTIC, CHILDREN'S PRESS, and associated logos are trademarks and/or registered trademarks of Scholastic Inc., 557 Broadway, New York, NY 10012.

Editor: Kate Moening   Designer: Andrea Schneider

Printed in the United States of America, North Mankato, MN.

Table of Contents

Who Is Sonia Sotomayor?   4

Getting Her Start   8

Changing the World   12

Sonia's Future   18

Glossary   22

To Learn More   23

Index   24

Who Is Sonia Sotomayor?

Sonia Sotomayor is a **justice** of the United States **Supreme Court**.

She is the court's first **Latina** justice!

U.S. Supreme Court Building

"LOOK AT THE GOOD IN PEOPLE... YOU'LL FIND LIFE MUCH MORE ENJOYABLE." (2015)

Sonia's parents were from Puerto Rico. They moved to New York City.

New York

New York City

Sonia's dad died when she was young. Her mom worked hard to care for the family.

Sonia loved reading. She wanted to solve mysteries. But at age 8, she learned she had **diabetes**.

Sonia's doctor told her
to pick a different job.
She decided to be a judge
after seeing one on television.

Sonia Sotomayor Profile

Birthday: June 25, 1954

Industry: law/government

Hometown: New York City
(Bronx), New York

Education:
- history degree
  (Princeton University)
- law degree (Yale Law School)

Influences and Heroes:
- Celina Baez Sotomayor (mother)
- José A. Cabranes (lawyer)
- Robert Morgenthau (lawyer;
  hired young Sonia)
- David Botwinik (lawyer;
  convinced Sonia to apply for her
  first judgeship)

Sonia studied history in college. Then she went to law school.

Sonia was a **prosecutor** before becoming a judge.

Princeton University, Sonia's college

Judge Sonia was tough but fair.

One of her **rulings** ended a baseball **strike**. People said she saved the sport!

In 1998, Sonia joined the **Court of Appeals**. She was always well prepared.

President Barack Obama chose her for the Supreme Court in 2009.

Sonia meeting with senators

Sonia with President Barack Obama

"THERE ARE TWO QUESTIONS I ASK MYSELF EVERY DAY. ONE IS: WHAT HAVE I LEARNED TODAY?... THE SECOND IS: WHO HAVE I HELPED TODAY?"
(2017)

Sonia had to work hard for the job. She met with many **senators**. She spent four days answering questions.

Sonia with Justices Ruth Bader Ginsburg and Elena Kagan

Sonia became the Supreme Court's third-ever woman justice!

From the Supreme Court, Sonia helps decide what the law means.

Sonia Sotomayor Timeline

1979   Sonia becomes a prosecutor in New York City

1992   Sonia becomes a judge of the U.S. District Court

1995   Sonia's ruling ends the 8-month-long Major League Baseball strike

1998   Sonia becomes a judge of the U.S. Court of Appeals

2009   Sonia becomes the 111th Justice of the Supreme Court on August 8

Sonia always speaks her mind. She fights for what is right!

Sonia **mentors** new law students. She speaks to Latino students and to children with diabetes.

Sonia shows people dreams can come true. She is a leader of the law!

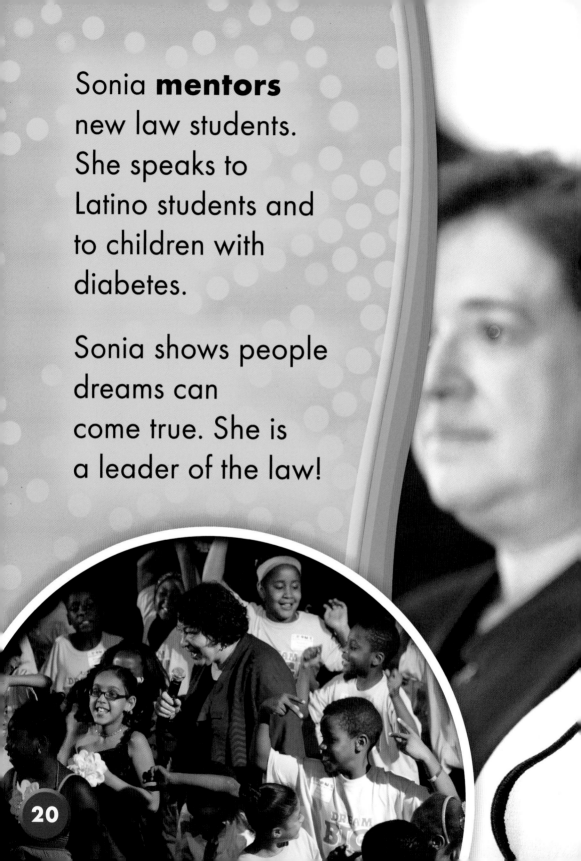

Glossary

Court of Appeals—a court that looks at other courts' decisions and decides if they were right

diabetes—a serious illness in which the body cannot control the amount of sugar in its blood

justice—a judge who serves on a higher court, such as the Supreme Court

Latina—having family roots from Central America, South America, or southern North America; Latina is the female form of Latino.

mentors—teaches or gives advice

prosecutor—a lawyer who tries to prove a case against someone accused of a crime

rulings—decisions made by a judge

senators—members of the Senate, a group that forms part of the United States Congress; it is a senator's job to make laws for the United States.

strike—a period of time in which workers stop work in order to force an employer to agree to their demands

Supreme Court—the highest court of law in the United States

To Learn More

AT THE LIBRARY

Kramer, Barbara. *Sonia Sotomayor*. Washington, D.C.: National Geographic, 2016.

Meltzer, Brad. *I Am Sonia Sotomayor*. New York, N.Y.: Dial Books for Young Readers, 2018.

Sotomayor, Sonia. *Turning Pages: My Life Story*. New York, N.Y.: Philomel Books, 2018.

ON THE WEB

FACTSURFER

Factsurfer.com gives you a safe, fun way to find more information.

1. Go to www.factsurfer.com.

2. Enter "Sonia Sotomayor" into the search box.

3. Click the "Surf" button and select your book cover to see a list of related web sites.

Index

baseball strike, 13
college, 10
Court of Appeals, 14
diabetes, 8, 20
family, 6, 7
judge, 9, 10, 12
justice, 4, 17
Latina, 4, 20
law, 18, 20
law school, 10
mentors, 20
New York City, 6, 7
Obama, Barack, 14, 15
profile, 9
prosecutor, 10
Puerto Rico, 6
quotes, 5, 11, 15
rulings, 13
senators, 14, 16

Supreme Court, 4, 14, 17, 18
timeline, 19
United States, 4

The images in this book are reproduced through the courtesy of: Steve Petteway/ Wikipedia, front cover (Sonia); Billion Photos, front cover (gavel); Nagel Photography, front cover (political chambers); StudioSmart, pp. 3, 22; Orhan Cam, p. 4 (inset); WENN Ltd / Alamy Stock Photo, pp. 4-5; The White House, p. 6; Rob Kim, pp. 8-9; AFP, p. 9 (inset); Spiroview Inc, p. 10 (inset); Mark Wilson, pp. 10-11; Allison Shelley, pp. 12-13 (top left); David Banks, pp. 12-13 (bottom right); Brooks Kraft, p. 14 (inset); Jewel Samad, pp. 14-15; Bloomberg, p. 16; Steve Petteway-Wikipedia, pp. 16-17 (top right); The State, pp. 18-19; Associated Press, p. 20 (inset); Allison Shelley, pp. 20-21.